HOT ROD PICTORIAL

featuring

DRY LAKES TIME TRIALS

compiled by

VEDA ORR

ANNOUNCEMENT

This book covers all S.C.T.A. records during the years of 1946, 1947, and 1948, when Hot Rod activities boomed on the dry lakes. It is not intended as a complete record book, but only as a description of the various cars and the unusual speeds attained in Hot Rod early days.

Copyright 1949

Published by

FLOYD CLYMER

World's Largest Publisher of Books Relating to Automobiles, Motorcycles, Motor Racing, and Americana

1268 SOUTH ALVARADO STREET, LOS ANGELES 6, CALIFORNIA

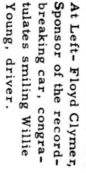

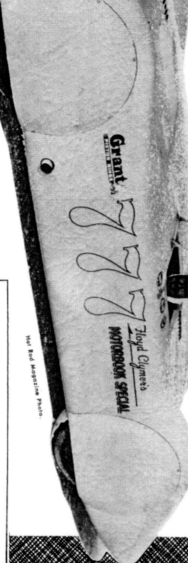

Foreword

Veda Orr was a pioneer in the early days of dry lakes racing. Known to most as the first female member of the Southern California Timing Association (S.C.T.A.) and the first woman to compete in S.C.T.A. racing, her life's accomplishments would later prove to be much more than simply these two achievements. Veda's passion drove her to take over the publishing of the S.C.T.A. Times, a racing newsletter started by Wally Parks. This small publication became an important piece of mail to racers who later fought overseas during World War II. It was Veda who mailed the newsletter to the soldiers at her own expense.

Fortunately, Veda also had an eye for photography. In this book, through photos and captions, she captures the essence of dry lakes hot rodding from 1946 through 1948, a time before corporate sponsorship and big paychecks. The photo of small trophies awarded for the 1946 season illustrates that early dry lakes' racing wasn't about money or prestige. It was about the men and women whose only focus was to go as fast as they possibly could in a race car that was, in many cases, built in their one car garage. Through the photo of 1946 S.C.T.A. officials that included a young Wally Parks among others, readers can imagine themselves rubbing elbows with those later to become icons of the sport.

Her book also brings to light the birth of the after-market parts industry. Photos illustrating Stuart Hilborn's early fuel injection system, Barney Navarro's experimental blower, Riley overhead valve conversions and hot cars powered by Iskenderian cams say more than words about the beginning of this emerging commercial enterprise.

Through her eyes, you'll see the story of racers who, with little money and no corporate catalog of speed parts, transform vehicles originally designed for a top speed of 50 to 60 mph; clock these same vehicles at more than double those speeds. Photos depict racers with their cars having been driven for hours to the lake beds, stripped of their fenders and hoods, raced, then re-assembled for the long drive home. Others, like Alex Xydias, thought out of the box when he built car #555 from the fuel tank of a World War II fighter plane.

Towards the end of the book, Veda adds exciting images of dry lakes and track cars pre-1946.Those images undoubtedly emphasize the mechanical and engineering skills of those who raced decades ago.

Considering *Veda Orr's New Revised Hot Rod Pictorial* has been out of print for nearly sixty-one years, it's a safe bet few of today's dry lakes racing enthusiasts have read or perhaps even heard of Veda Orr's book. But thanks to VelocePress, a new generation of racing fans now has the opportunity to experience those exciting early days on the lake beds through her eyes.

Joe Babiasz ~ November 2010

For those readers interested in learning more about
the early history of hot rodding and land speed racing
and to keep up with current events, we encourage
you to visit the following websites.

The official website of the S.C.T.A.

www.scta-bni.org

You will find all of the latest news plus information on upcoming events.

The official website of the SLSRH

(Society of Land Speed Racing Historians)

www.landspeedracing.com

You will find both current and historical information relating to
land speed racing.

A review of Veda Orr's '46 *LAKES PICTORIAL*, which was expanded to include data from '47 & '48 and published in 1949 by Floyd Clymer as *Veda Orr's New Revised HOT ROD PICTORIAL*.

I always wondered why Veda Orr held a special place in the hearts and minds of nearly every dry lakes racer from the 1940's. My father, Wally Parks, knew the Orr's quite well and he always respected them for what they contributed to dry lakes racing and hot rodding in general. Veda was the first woman to be allowed to race in the SCTA, and that was as much due to the love and respect that the racers had for her as it was for the position and reputation of her husband, Karl Orr. As World War II began in late December 1941 and early 1942, the dry lakes land speed community lost their young men, who were drafted or enlisted and sent overseas. I interviewed many of these veterans years after the war ended and nearly all of them believed that they were not coming home alive. In this depressed mindset Veda wrote to them with the news of the local racing scene to lift their spirits and keep them focused on doing their job of winning the war and returning home to loved ones and the dry lakes they loved to race on.

So great was her correspondence list that she created a newsletter format, mimeographed it at her expense and sent this newsletter off to whoever wrote to her. She expanded her enterprise by finding the addresses of every land speed racer that she could find and kept this up for years, until the war was over and the boys came home. We shouldn't forget Karl Orr, for every step that Veda took, her husband stood firmly behind her with financial support and encouragement. The *Lakes Pictorial* was one of her last endeavors and it did very well, but within a few more years she and Karl would be involved in oval track racing and then a divorce would end their racing partnership. Veda and Karl had no children; racing was the thread that bound them together and when that was severed they drifted apart. Veda raced on the dry lakes under the sanction of the Southern California Timing Association (SCTA) when all women were banned. It was thought that females could not safely control the growing horsepower and the increasing speeds and would surely crash. Such injuries or possible deaths would cause negative publicity in the press and drive the public into the arms of crusaders who wanted to end all racing, legal or otherwise.

Fear is what drove the SCTA to ban women as members and racers in their organization. It was a fear based on fact, because illegal street racing before and after WWII was causing a backlash. Laws and bills were being raised in Sacramento and legislators were under pressure to stop the carnage on the roads caused by illegal street racing. Veda was no ordinary woman though. She was cool and collected in Karl's famed roadster and she could flat out beat many of the men. It helped that Karl Orr stood behind her every inch of the way. You can't separate Veda from Karl Orr. They could survive and thrive on their own, but together they made an impressive couple. Veda was good for Karl's business, but Karl was able to free Veda from the constraints of her gender. No one chose to take on Karl Orr. He was an imposing figure and 10 to 15 years older than the average racer. He had the experience and the political might to sway most of the SCTA and other dry lakes timing associations to his will.

Karl also enjoyed breaking the rules when it suited him and he did not like to be told what to do or how to do it. When he put Veda in the drivers seat he was telling the other officials that he could and would do what he wanted. It simply didn't pay to take on Karl Orr and it would have been too divisive to try. Veda Orr on the other hand was not only charming, beautiful and a skilled driver, she also won over the hearts and minds of the other racers. Maybe most of the men were opposed to her racing before the war, but the long and desperate war changed their way of thinking, especially after receiving all those letters and newsletters from Veda. Veda didn't pull any punches or mislead anyone; they got the news straight up. After the war it was hard to find anyone who wanted to oppose Karl or say no to Veda. Maybe a few tried, but men like Ak Miller, Randy Shinn, Wally Parks and other influential men simply owed too much to Veda to say no to her. A vote of the club representatives made Veda a special member, one with driving privileges. This was no small step either, for women were not only banned from racing, they were banned from the club meetings. This was a male institution, with only one exception, Veda Orr.

I feel the same way about *Lakes Pictorial* as an archeaologist would feel if they found the ancient Rosetta Stone or the burial site of Saint Peter or Paul. The book isn't much, in fact it's rather small, but it represents the very beginnings of our sport of land speed racing and thus, by and in itself, this is a historical part of our heritage. As a historical aid it is very important. They list some of the racers who made important contributions to land speed racing, including Art Tilton, Ernie McAfee, Jack McGrath, Manuel Ayulo, Bruce Blair and others. Bruce of course was killed in an airplane crash over the desert, and Nellie Taylor was recovering from severe war injuries that would shorten his life. Danny Sakai was killed in an auto accident. The first photograph shows Veda Orr in the 7C Karl Orr Speed Shop Special, recording a speed of 121.62 in the Class C roadsters, in May, 1947. The title says *Veda Orr's Lakes Pictorial 1946 Season*, but here we have a photo from 1947. Sometimes the captions get a bit sloppy. She follows that photograph with three more of her, one at Kearney-Mesa in San Diego in 1938. A rather famous photo shows the SCTA officials meeting with Rex Mays, Louie Meyer, Addie Leonard and DeRalph Frizzell at a MacMillan Petroleum meeting in 1946. The SCTA representatives included Wally Parks, Mel Leighton and Randy Shinn.

The drawings by Richard (Dick) Teague can be found in SCTA Programs and in the SCTA Racing News, but here is another opportunity to own some of

Teague's drawings. There were quite a few talented artists and drawers during the early days and often when a camera wasn't available, a free hand sketch recorded the run. A photograph of the SCTA awards presented at the banquet in 1946 includes a caption remark that the trophies were designed by Gus Maanum, another very talented artist and sketcher. Veda then shows all but 15 of the 58 cars that won the right to carry their numbers into the next season. They read like a who's who of dry lakes racers; the very Holy Grail of the sport. The first is Randy Shinn who was leading the points championship until seriously injured in an accident that left a huge scar from scalp to chin. Shinn was out of the running and that left Tony Capanna with a chance to get the points necessary to win the season's individual points championship. Tony turned his car over to another driver rather than win in an uneven race. Don Blair earned enough points to send Tony down to 3rd place, but the members of the SCTA were so impressed that they voted Capanna the first recipient of the Art Tilton Sportsmanship trophy.

Kenny Lindley took fourth, followed by Stuart Hilborn, then Doug Carruthers, Howard Wilson, Karl Orr, Lou Baney and the Schiefer/Theodorelus car. In eleventh place was Charles Scott, then Jack Calori, Bob Smithson, Chuck Potvin, Palm Brothers/Doug Hartelt, Bill Burke, Charles Gregory, Dick Kraft, Phil Remington and Harold Anderson. Kraft would make a name for himself in early drag racing and Remington in road racing. Veda Orr would place number 21 in points that season, followed by Kenneth Jones, Jack McGrath, Bert Letner, Frank Coon, Dick Neville, Arnold Birner, Lowell Lewis, Jim Harrell and Yam Oka. Weiand/Van Maanen placed 31st in the points race, followed by Palm Brothers, Manuel (Manny) Ayulo, Steve Genardini, Archie Tipton, R.L. Shinn (in his second car), John Cannon and Richard Allen. The 39th place was not assigned and there is no reason given. John McCoy took the 40th place in the standings, followed by Bruno Salazar, Marvin Lee, Al Deverich, Bill Brown, Chauncey Crist, Harry Oka, Bob Speik, Thun Brothers, Porrazzo Brothers, and Terry Smith. In spot number 51 was Bob Riese and then came Gilbert Ayala, A. W. Barrett, Bob Hill, Gold/Lee, Bruce Blair, Bub Marcia and George Barber.

All but fifteen of these men and one woman have their cars shown in *Lakes Pictorial*. The last six pages show other well-known dry lakes racers who finished out of the points chase or who didn't participate in racing that year. Danny Sakai had passed away and Bob Rufi gave up racing after his near fatal accident. Rufi set the dry lakes racing community on its head with a pre-war run that broke 140 miles per hour. A great many racers reached for that record, but Rufi was the first in his little hand-built streamliner. Also mentioned are Sandy Belond, Spalding Brothers, Ralph Schenck, Vern Houle, Roscoe Turner, Ed Iskenderian, John Athans and Jim Nairn. The last photograph in the *Lakes Pictorial* is Veda and Karl Orr. Why not, they financed and created this little gem and they deserve to have the front and back pages all to themselves. Karl is seated in his 1942 record holding modified which won the points championship that year. Veda is standing beside her husband. Karl has a rare smile and a ruggedly handsome face partly hidden by his helmet. Veda has a radiant smile in her helmet and cover-alls. For that brief moment there was no one quite as beautiful as Veda Orr and it is easy to see why the land speed guys fell in love with her. She was at the top of her world.

There is a brief introductory page mentioning the Southern California Timing Association (SCTA) members who are still in the military and have not been released from active duty in World War II, and Veda and Karl Orr are mentioned as the creators of the pamphlet. At the time it was simply a labor of love for Veda and there was little thought of economic gain or that this raw pamphlet would ever have more than a short lifespan. There are 12 black and white drawings by Richard (Dick) Teague and 83 black and white photographs.

Richard Parks ~ Editor of the Society of Land Speed Racing Historians Newsletter (Newsletter website: www.landspeedracing.com)

FOOTNOTE: Clymer's *Veda Orr's New Revised HOT ROD PICTORIAL* contains 8 black and white drawings by Richard (Dick) Teague and 102 black and white photographs.

The following information was provided by Jim Miller~ President of the Society of Land Speed Racing Historians:

The original *Lakes Pictorial* was copyrighted by Veda in 1947 and was saddle stitched. Floyd Clymer published an updated and enlarged version of this book with a different cover and more pages it was titled *Hot Rod Pictorial* and copyrighted by Clymer in 1949. In the late '80's, Jim Lattin, then president of the S.C.T.A., republished a version of Veda's '46 *Lakes Pictorial*. Finally what may be thought to be a typo is not, in the description that accompanies the photo of DANNY SAKAI'S modified, Ord is the correct spelling, Mal Ord made cylinder heads among other parts for Ford flatheads and is a legend among dry lakes historians.

Jim Lattin's '46 Lakes Pictorial reprint can be purchased at: http://scta-bni.org

TERMINOLOGY: To help some of our readers who were too young to have been around the Lakes in the '40's we include the following explanation submitted by Bob Falcon:

Perhaps I can shed some light on some of the descriptive language we hot rodders used in the late 1940s, which is when Veda published her Lakes Pictorials. I don't think she published very many but I still have the one she gave me in my library. I was in high school at the time and was a regular visitor to the Speed Shop she and Karl operated that was located across the street from the 'Culver City Roller Rink'...about a half block from the 'Piccadilly's Drive In' that was a magnet for hot rods every Saturday night. I also used to visit their home quite often since it was located very close to where my folks lived in Culver City. Karl was also a regular at my dad's wheel alignment shop located across Washington Blvd from MGM Studios.

My parent's house on La Salle Avenue and the Orr residence on Keystone Avenue were both located on the site of the old Culver City Board Speedway of the 1920s. The one and one-half mile speedway was located south of Braddock Drive on the north, Keystone on the west, La Salle on the east and Ballona Creek on the south. The distance between the Orr's and the Falcon's was a mere five residential blocks.

Back then all Fords were referred to as "V8's" unless they were four cylinder Fords which were called "As", "Bs" or "T's". Therefore, the reference in the caption identifying the vehicle as an "Ord V8" is correct as it was a <u>Ford</u> crafted by Mal <u>Ord</u> who worked for the Don Lee organization and built several cars for the Auto Dealer owner. Another interesting note is that the preferred models of Fords were the even numbered years beginning in 1932 and stopping at 1936 with a jump to 1940. If you check some photos of the convertibles during those model years they were more attractive than their odd year counterparts.

While I was a student Alexander Hamilton High School I helped John Kelly build a Track Roadster that he raced at Culver City Speedway and several other oval tracks in the LA area. He raced with an organization named California Sports Cars that was formed by Tony Coldaway and raced in competition to the California Roadster Association (CRA). Many do not know that there were three, or four, oval track Roadster racing associations operating in Los Angeles in addition to groups at Bakersfield, Fresno and Oakland.

In latter years, at the insistence of my late friend Jerry Bondio, we began to compete in the S.C.T.A. 'F Production Class', using my 1992 Ford Taurus SHO. Jerry was an old Rusetta lakes racer so we did some tricks to the SHO and earned the SCTA Muroc Class record in my "daily driver" that was driven up to the lake bed, like the Lakes Racers of the 1940's.

FOOTNOTE: Bob Falcon hails from an early day Eastern racing family and has been a participant in So Cal racing since the 1940s. His current vocation is a racing historian and writer.

Veda Orr is the only woman member of the Southern California Timing Association. She has been driving Roadsters, Modifieds and Streamliners since 1937 on the Dry Lakes of California. Her best time was 132 m.p.h., officially timed on Rosamond Dry Lake, California.

1946 S.C.T.A. OFFICIALS -- Front row, left to right: Wally Parks, SCTA President; Mel Leighton, SCTA Treasurer; Randy Shinn, SCTA Secretary. Standing, left to right: 'Addie' Leonard, expert on motor mechanics; DeRalph Frizell, Macmillan's Chief Engineer; Lou Meyer, 3-time winner of the Indianapolis Memorial Day 500-Mile Classic; Rex Mays, AAA Champion. Photo taken at demonstration by Macmillan Petroleum Refinery.

A fine display of trophies awarded for the 1946 season. First place trophies are gold finished; second place, silver; third, fourth and fifth places, bronze. Trophies designed by Gus Maanum. --*J. Allen Hawkins photo*

SOUTHERN CALIFORNIA TIMING ASSOCIATION

SEASON CHAMPIONS

1938	ERNIE McAFEE	(Road Runners)
1939	GEORGE HARVEY	(Road Runners)
1940	BOB RUFI	(Albata)
1941	VIC EDELBROCK	(Road Runners)
1942	KARL ORR	(Albata)
1946	RANDY SHINN	(Road Runners)
1947	DOUG HARTELT tied with DIETRICH & THOMAS	(Lancers) (Gaters)
1948	SPURGIN & GIOVANINE (Albata)	

Part I of the Revised Hot Rod Pictorial deals with the cars which ran at the 'Dry Lakes' during the 1946 Season. During that season cars were divided into four classes, as follows:

Roadster	-	engines up to 260 cu. in.
Modified	-	engines up to 260 cu. in.
Streamliner	-	engines up to 260 cu. in.
Unlimited	-	any chassis, engines over 260 cu. in.

Record holders:

Roadster	-	RANDY SHINN	(Road Runner)	128.66 mph
Modified	-	KARL ORR	(Albata)	133.03 mph
Streamliner	-	BOB RUFI	(Albata)	140.00 mph
Unlimited	-	TONY CAPANNA	(Albata)	137.24 mph

The following cars were some of the point winners of the 1947 season at the 'Lakes' under S.C.T.A. Sanction. The cars are numbered and listed according to points earned during the 1946 season.

Car No. 1 - RANDY SHINN (Road Runner) Won SCTA 1946 Championship. Totaled 75 Points for Season. Roadster record holder - 128.66 mph average (132.74 one way). Model 'T' Channelled job.

Car No. 2 - DON BLAIR (Gopher) totaled 74 Points for Season. Unlimited class - Best time for 1946, 141.06 mph. Engine: '46 Merc. Standard stroke, 3 5/16 bore, Roots blower, Denver heads Weiand manifold, Harman cam.

Car No. 3 - TONY CAPANNA (Albata) totaled 68
points for Season. Unlimited class record
holder 137.24 mph average 2-way run. (145.39 mph
one way -- fastest time ever clocked at any
SCTA Dry Lake meet) 16 Cyl. Marmon,- Harman

No. 4 - KENNY LINDLEY (Lancers) 63 points.
Best time for 1946 - 128.93 mph in Modified
Class. Engine: '32 Ford, Standard Merc bore,
Meyer heads, Evans Manifold, Smith cam, 3.27
gears, 6.00 x 16 tires.

No. 5 - STUART HILBORN (Centuries) Streamliner. Fastest time 139.96 mph. With Stu in
the upper left is Eddie Miller, designer of the
manifold, exhaust system and cam, which he
ground by file and grindstone, taking several
months to finish. Miller is an Indianapolis man,
known for his thoroughness and patience. In '21
he finished 4th at the '500' where he Captained
the Duesenberg team. He serves on the AAA Tech-
nical Committee for the Bonneville Salt Flat
record runs. Next page shows the carburetion
and the Streamliner itself. Totaled 48 points
for the Season.

More pictures of Stuart Hilborn's
Streamliner. Manifold and carburetors shown at upper left. Note
small frontal area in photo below.

Car No. 6 - DOUG CARUTHERS (Road Runners)
Modified class. Totaled 45 points for Season.
Best time '46 - 130.81 mph. Runs a stroked Merc
engine.

Car No. 7 - HOWARD WILSON (Low Flyers) Ran
three different chassis, roadster and two modifieds. Totaled 42 points for Season. Best
roadster time 123.96 mph. Best modified time
140.40 mph, but failed to break the present
modified record.

Car No. 8 - KARL ORR (Albata) Won SCTA Championship in '42, held it through '46. Standing
modified record holder 133.03 mph average. 1940
Merc engine, Bertrand cam, filled heads. Best
time 1946 127.65 mph. Totaled 39 points for
season.

Car No. 9 - LOUIS BANEY (Gopher) Totaled 33
points 1946. Best time 122.61 mph. Engine Merc
1/4 in. stroked, Offenhauser heads and manifold,
Winfield cam, Spalding ignition.

Car No. 11 - CHARLES SCOTT (Hornets) Totaled
32 points for Season. Fastest time 123.28 mph
Metal sprayed crank - 3/16 in. stroker.

Car No. 12 - JACK CALORI (Lancers) Totaled 28
points - Fastest time 123.28 mph. '40 Merc
engine, 3 5/16 bore, 1/8 in. stroke, Meyers
heads, Weiand manifold, Smith cam, 3.54 gears,
7.00 tires.

Car No. 13 - BOB SMITHSON (Pasadena Roadster
Club) Totaled 26 points. Fastest time 128.40
mph. '40 Merc engine, 3 5/16 bore, 1/8 in. stroke,
Edelbrock heads and manifold, Smith cam, Potvin
ignition, 3.54 gears, 7.00 tires.

Car No. 14 - CHUCK POTVIN (Lancers) Totaled 22 points. Best time 126.76 mph. '40 Merc, 3 5/16 bore, 1/8 in. stroke, Edelbrock heads, Evans manifold, Smith cam, 3.54 gears, 7.00 tires.

Car No. 15 - PALM BROS. - HARTELT (Lancers) Totaled 22 points. Fastest time 123.28 mph. Rear engine car, '41 Merc, 3 5/16 bore, stock stroke, Evans manifold, Denver heads, Smith cam, 3.27 gears.

Car No. 16 - BILL BURKE (Road Runner) ED
KORGAN, driver, beside belly tank Streamliner.
Fastest time in 1946 131.96 mph.

Car No. 18 - DICK KRAFT (Lancers) Fastest time
in 1946 120.00 mph. 'T' - V8 Roadster.

Car No. 19 - PHIL REMINGTON (Low Flyers) This
modified went 125.52 for the best time in '46.

Car No. 20 - HAROLD ANDERSON (Gopher) Fastest
time in 1946 122.95 mph. '42 Merc engine with
Edelbrock equipment.

Car No. 21 - VEDA ORR (Albata) Best time '46 122.78 mph. '42 Merc engine, Meyer heads, Navarro manifold, Harman cam, Potvin ignition.

Car No. 23 - JACK McGRATH (Gophers) Last season Jack ran a '32 Roadster which he clocked at 123.96 mph. Equipped with a Merc engine, big bore and stroke, Evans manifold. Above photo is the 'T'-Merc that he now runs on the track.

Car No. 25 - FRANK COON (Low Flyers) Fastest
time 1946 122.78. Merc engine stroked, filled
heads, Evans manifold, Engle cam, Coon ignition.

Car No. 27 - ARNOLD BIRNER (Bungholer) Modified Class. Best time '46: 126.93 mph 4-port
Riley.

Car No. 29 - JIM HARRELL (Albata) Modified
class. Fastest time '46: 126.40 mph. Harrell
heads and manifold, Spalding ignition, Winfield
full race cam.

Car No. 31 - WEIAND - VAN MAANEN (Outriders)
'42 Merc stroked 1/8 in., bored 3 5/16. Weber
3/4 cam, Weiand heads and manifold, '27 'T'
roadster body, 3.78 gears, 7.00 x 16 tires.
This job is also being run on the roadster
tracks.

Car No. 36 - R. L. SHINN (Road Runner) Merc
engine. Best time in 1946: 121.13 mph.

Car No. 45 - CHAUNCEY CRIST (Lancers) Rear-
engine V8, Meyer set-up. Fastest time '46:
118.57 mph.

Car No. 51 - BOB RIESE (Gear Grinders) Ford
V8, High altitude heads. Best time 1946:
118.11 mph.

Car No. 58 - GEORGE BARBER (Southern California Roadster Club) Al Jerauld, standing.
Fastest time '46: 117.18 mph. Merc engine,
stroked and bored, Meyer's heads, Navarro manifold, Smith cam, 3.54 gears, 7.00 x 16 tires.

End of Part I of the revised Hot Rod Pictorial. This section has shown the cars that ran at the lakes in 1946 and their relative positions at the end of that year.

An album of drawings by Richard (Dick) Teague follows, these drawings appeared in S.C.T.A. programs and in the S.C.T.A. Racing News.

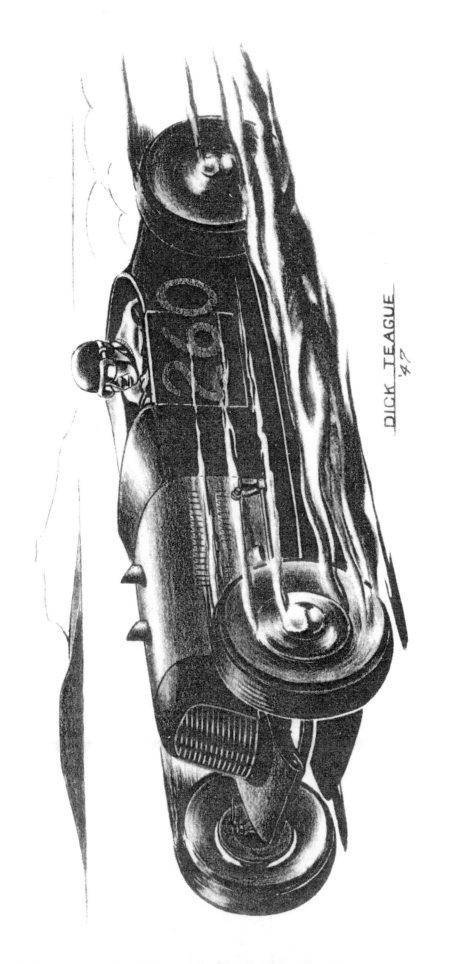

DICK TEAGUE '47

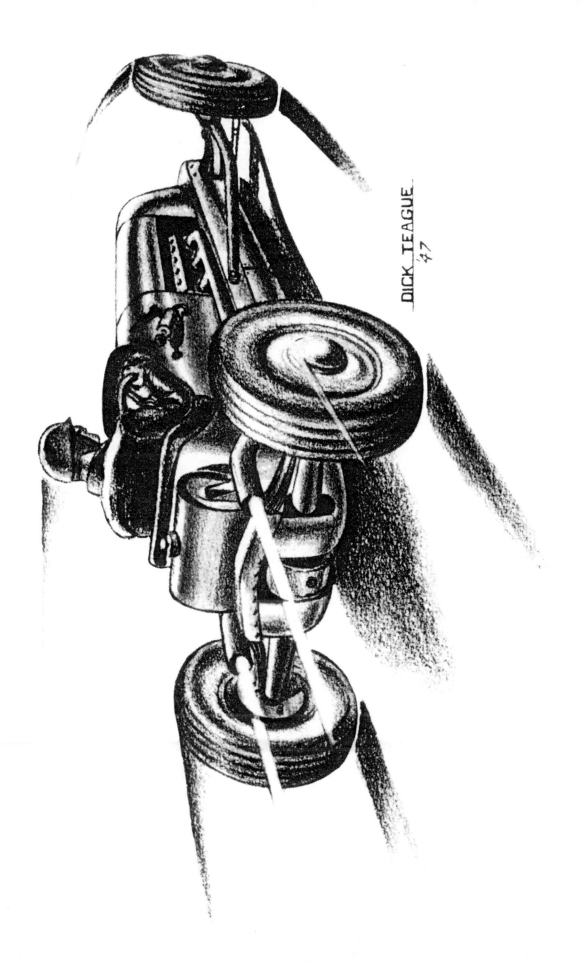

DICK TEAGUE
'47

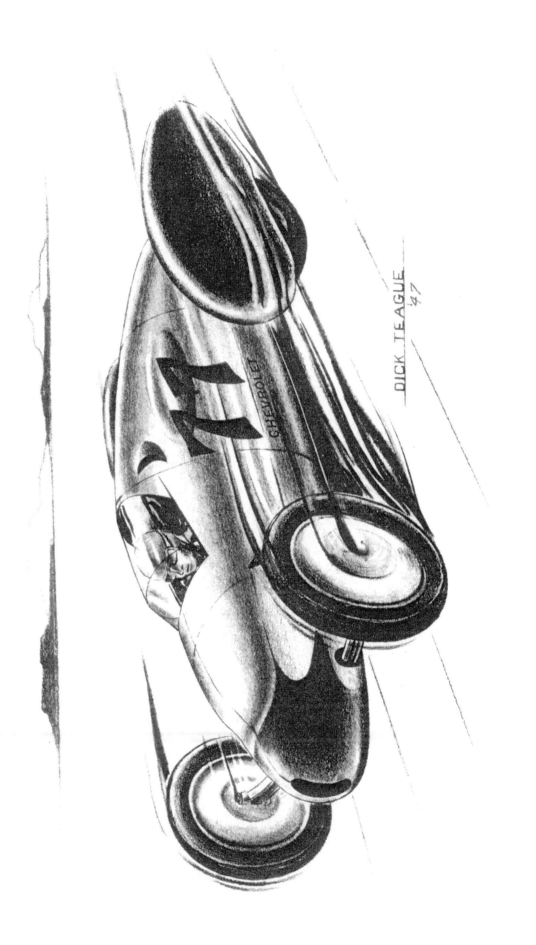

CHEVROLET

DICK TEAGUE '47

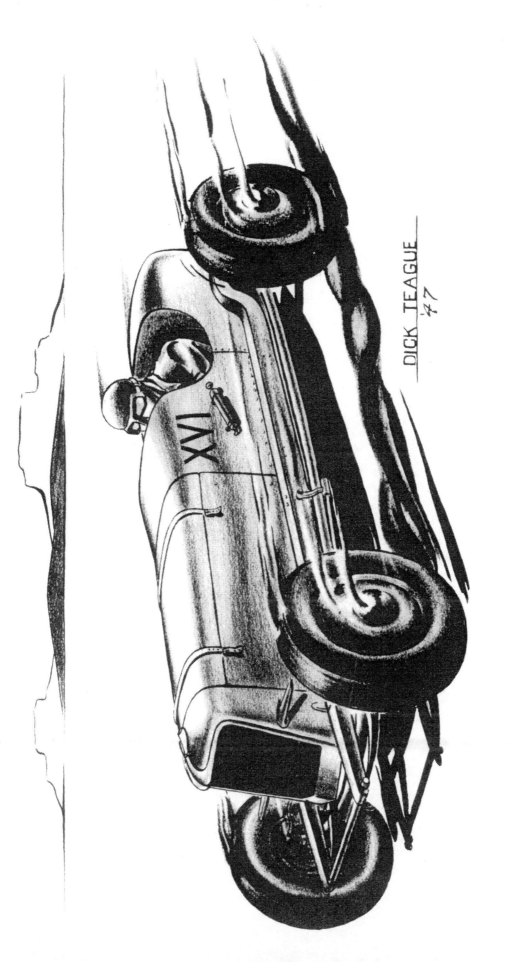

DICK TEAGUE '47

DICK TEAGUE
'47

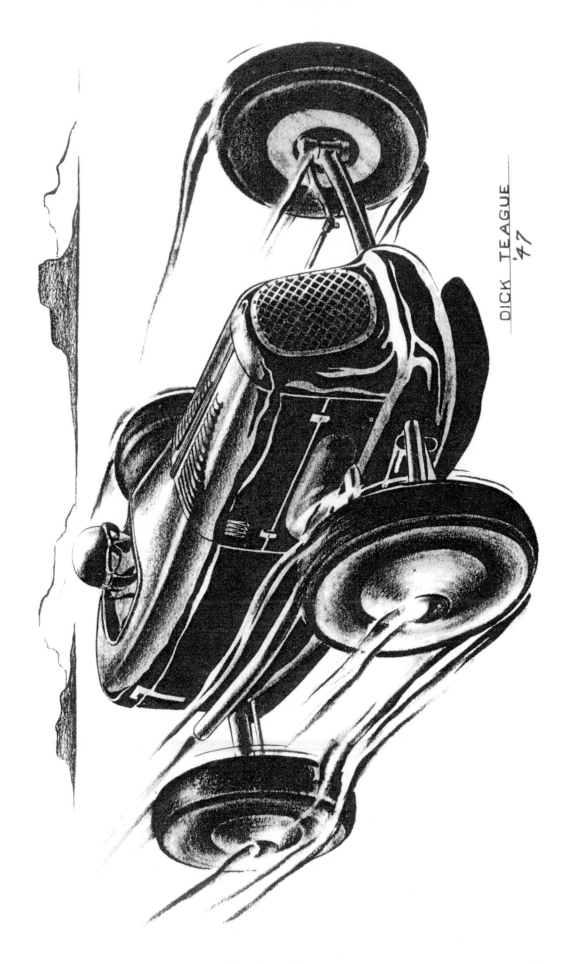

DICK TEAGUE '47

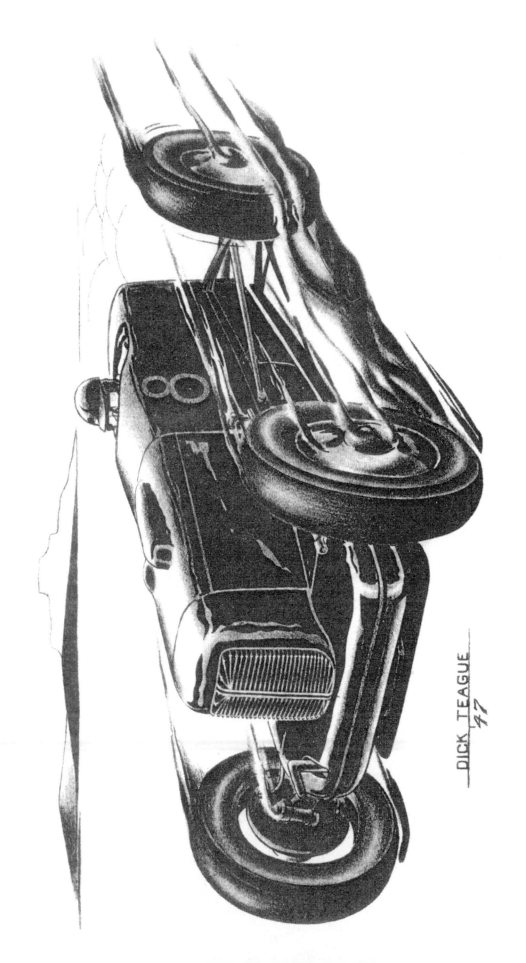

DICK TEAGUE '47

DICK TEAGUE '47

Part II, which follows, shows the cars that ran during the 1947 season. In 1947 the S.C.T.A. introduced a new system of classification, with all cars classed as either ROADSTERS or STREAM-LINERS, thus eliminating the 'Modified' class. The all-time standing modified record of 133.03 mph average is held by Karl Orr.

There are four classes for each of the two body types, divided according to Engine Displacement thus:

Class A -   0 to 150 cubic inches
Class B -   150 to 250 cubic inches
Class C -   250 to 350 cubic inches
Class D -   350 cubic inches, and over

The time that each car made is given in the caption accompanying each picture.

Typical 'Race Day' crowd at the 'Lakes'. Evidence of the increasing popularity of the Dry Lakes events among Southern California fans, Race Day has seen even a few visitors from New York, Chicago and Florida.

'BLACKIE' GOLD (Pasadena Roadster Club) No. 55 - Class 'C' Roadster, clocked at 122.78 mph Sept. 1947. '42 Merc engine, Edelbrock heads, Evans manifold, Harman cam, Evans ignition.

AK MILLER (Road Runner member - S.C.T.A.
President) No. 115 - Class 'B' Roadster, Clocked
106.25 mph, July 1947. Buick 8 engine, stock
head and manifold, Winfield cam.

'MULTY' ALDRICH - PASSER entry (Hornets)
No. 290 - Class 'B' Roadster. Clocked 87.54 mph,
Sept. 1947. 1922 Ford 'T' Roadster, '22 Ford
'T' engine, Rajo head and manifold, 'Multy'
cam, Nash dual ignition.

ALAN HALL (Sidewinders) No. 317. Class 'B'
Streamliner, clocked 116.88 mph Oct. 1947. '45
Ford V8 engine, Alexander head, Edelbrock mani-
fold, engle cam, magneto.

JOHNNY JOHNSON (Road Runners) No. 104 Class
'B' Roadster, clocked 127.11 mph Sept. 1947.
Model 'T' chassis, Merc engine, Navarro heads
and manifold, Winfield cam.

ARNOLD BIRNER (Throttlers) No. 27, Class 'B'
Streamliner, clocked 134.73 mph Oct. 1947. Rear-
engine 'drop tank', Ford 'B' '32 engine, Riley
4-port head, Spl. manifold, Riley cam, Spl.igni-
tion.

JACK AVAKIAN (Road Runner) No. 112, Class 'B'
Streamliner, clocked 128.38 mph Sept. 1947.
'Drop tank' streamliner, Merc engine, Navarro
heads, Edelbrock manifold, Smith cam.

DIETRICH-THOMAS entry (Gaters) Driven by Ed
Hulse. No. 657 Class 'C' Streamliner. Held
record for this class Sept. 1947 at 138.46 mph
average. Fastest time clocked 139.31 - Oct. 1947.
Engine: '40 Merc, Navarro heads & manifold, Smith
cam, Wico mag.

JACK McAFEE (Throttlers) No. 431 Class 'C'
Streamliner, clocked 114.79 mph Sept. 1947. Car
also raced on tracks under WRA banner. Ford 'B'
engine, D. O. Hal head, McAfee cam and manifold.

MARC CRAVENS (Idlers) No. 441 Class 'B' Roadster, clocked 110.70 mph Oct. 1947. Ford 'B'
engine, Fargo 4-port head, Spl. manifold, Smith
cam, own spl. ignition.

BRISTOL-WOODSIDE entry (Albata) No. 97 Class
'C' Streamliner, clocked 123.28 mph July 1947.
'Drop Tank', Ford V8 engine, Offenhauser heads
and manifold.

DON NICHOLSON (Glendale Strokers) No. 557 Class
'B' Roadster, clocked 120.48 mph Aug. 1947.
Chevy 6 engine, Chevy head, Own spl. manifold,
Harman cam, own spl. ignition.

WILLIAM GIRTON (Chi-Winders) No. 725. Guest
from Chicago. Class 'C' Roadster clocked 96.05
mph Aug. 1947.

BERT LETNER'S 'Elco Twin' Engine. Note dual spark plugs. (Car pictured below)

BERT LETNER (Road Runners) No. 24 Class 'C' Roadster driven at Lakes by Art Lamey. Car also driven on tracks by Troy Ruttman. Clocked 125.87 July 1947. Merc engine, Elco Twin heads, Edelbrock manifold, Smith cam, Elco ignition.

53

Class B Roadster - 126.17 mph average.
DOUG HARTELT (Lancers Club) ('46 Merc,
Meyer Heads, Navarro manifold, Smith cam,
Potvin Ignition)

Class B Streamliner - 136.39 mph average.
JOHNSON-CARUTHERS (Road Runners Club) ('46 Merc,
Navarro heads and manifold, Smith cam, Kurten
Ignition)

Class C Roadster - 136.05 mph average.
REGG SCHLEMMER (Gaters Club) ('47 Merc,
Navarro heads, Evans manifold, Smith cam,
Magneto)

Class C Streamliner - 139.21 mph average.
BILL BURKE (Road Runners Club) (Merc, Weiand
heads and manifold, Weber cam, Spalding Ign.)

Class D Roadster - 130.76 mph average.
RANDY SHINN (Road Runners Club) ('39 Merc,
Edelbrock heads and manifold, Winfield
cam, Edelbrock Ignition)

End of Part II, of the revised Hot Rod Pictorial. This section has shown the cars that
ran at the lakes in the 1947 season.

Part III, which follows, shows the cars that
ran at the lakes in the 1948 season.

BOB WENZ (Low Flyers) No. 38, Class 'B' Roadster. Clocked 128.22 mph July 1948. '29 Ford 'A' frame, '27 'T' body, '32 Ford V8 engine, Ford heads filled, Weiand manifold, Engle cam, Coon ignition.

JIM GUPTILL (Lancers) No. 110, Class 'B' Roadster Clocked 129.12 mph April 1948. '41 Merc eng., Evans heads and manifold, Smith cam, Potvin ignition.

LLOYD KEAR (Mobilers) No. 33, Class 'B' Roadster. Clocked 131.19 April 1948. Essex frame,
'24 'T' body, '42 Ford V8 engine, Meyers heads
Spalding manifold, cam and ignition.

CHARLES CLARK (Clutchers) No. 435, Class 'B'
Roadster. Clocked 122.61 mph July 1948. '29
Ford 'A' frame and body, '46 Ford V8 engine,
Cyclone heads, Evans manifold, Smith cam, own
special ignition.

One of the few Riley Overheads for V8s.

NELSON MORRIS No. 909, Class 'B' Roadster
(Hot Rod Show-built car, Guest entry) Clocked
105.63 mph June 1948. '46 Merc engine, Evans
heads, Navarro manifold, Weber cam, Kong ignition.

Close-up of the experimental Navarro blower
manifold and drive used in car No. 240 below.

TOM BEATTY - B. J. NAVARRO (Glendale Strokers)
No. 240, Class 'C' Roadster. Clocked 121.29
mph July 1948. '41 Ford V8, Navarro heads,
Navarro super-charger, Winfield cam, Kurten
ignition.

SPURGIN-GIOVANINE (Albata) No. 15, Class 'A' Roadster. Fastest time, one way 123.79 mph July 1948. Record holder (for class) as of Sept. 1948 at 123.05 mph average. '25 Chevrolet 4 engine, Olds head, spl. manifold, Winfield cam, Mallory ignition. At each meet during 1948 these members have broken their own previous record.

PAUL SCHIEFER (So.Calif. Rdstr. Club) No. 315, Class 'C' Roadster, clocked 148.02 July 1948. '46 Merc engine, '25 'T' body, Tubular frame, Edelbrock heads and manifold, Harman cam, Meyer ignition.

ALEX XYDIAS (Sidewinders) No. 555, Class 'A'
Streamliner. Fastest time, one way, 131.19 mph
July 1948. Record holder (for class) as of July 1948
at 129.05 mph average for two-way run. '39 V8 '60'
engine, Edelbrock heads and manifold, Winfield cam,
Spalding ignition. Car is a 'wing tank' with rear
engine, and is painted gold and white.

JOHN COLLINS (San Diego Rdstr. Club) No. 337, Class 'B' Roadster, clocked 125.17 mph July 1948. '26 Model 'T' body on '32 Ford frame, '46 Merc engine, Edelbrock heads, Navarro manifold, Bertrand cam, Spalding ignition.

SPALDING BROTHERS (Mobilers) No. 260, Class 'B' Roadster, clocked 127.65 mph July 1948. '27 'T' Roadster chassis constructed by John Hartman, features torsion bar suspension on all four wheels, Stelling gear box and late Chevrolet differential. '41 Chevrolet 6 engine, 248 cu. ins., Wayne head and manifold, Bill Spalding billet cam, Tom Spalding ignition.

This concludes Part III of the Revised Hot Rod Pictorial. Part IV, which follows, features photographs taken prior to the 1946 Season, unless otherwise specified.

SPALDING BROTHERS' V8 Streamliner.
Clocked 127.48 in 1939.

Another view of the Spalding Streamliner.
Note the air-scoop at the front end.

KARL ORR Modified, Cragar engine clocked
125.35 in 1939.

The West-Rubsch streamlined 'Skipit'
with a Cragar engine did 114.74 in 1940.

One of the first 'belly pan' roadsters at
the lakes. - 1941

DANNY SAKAI'S Modified. Ord V8 set-up clocked
125.52 in 1941.

MAL ORD made cylinder heads and other
parts for Ford Flatheads - Jim Miller).

BOB RUFI (Albata) Streamliner
record holder -- 140.00 mph average.
4 cylinder Chevrolet, 3-port head,
rear engine.

RALPH SCHENK'S Streamliner. Powered by a 186 cu. in.
Chevrolet 4, Winfield carburetion and cam. Best time pre-
war days 126.89 mph. In 1946 Paul Harestad owned the car.

VERNE HOULE (Road Runners) English
Riley V8 Modified clocked about
126.00 mph.

SPALDING BROTHERS' Modified. Riley Overhead
V8 with Roots 'Blower'.

ED ISKENDERIAN (Idlers) '25 'T'-V8 with overheads (reclaimed Maxi heads), and Winfield cam.
Clocked by Western Timing in 1941 at 120 mph.

BOB BERKSHIRE (Idlers) (car not yet timed
when picture taken) '46 Merc, Visel pistons,
Edmunds heads, Weiand manifold, Harman super
cams, special body by Berkshire with tubular
frame. Cost $2,000, not counting one year's
labor.

JIM NAIRN (Idlers) Merc engine, Weiand manifold, Denver heads, Smith cam. Clocked in 1946
at 116 mph.

This is NOT (believe it or not) another
picture of the car above, but a shot of John
Athans' car. Merc engine, Winfield cam, Athans
heads. Clocked 109 pre-war.

Part V of the Hot Rod Pictorial, which follows, features some of the track jobs which have been running in Southern California during the past seasons.

JACK McGRATH'S track job. '27 'T' Roadster
'46 Merc engine, Meyers heads, Winfield cam,
Evans manifold & ignition, 4:11 ratio, Stelling
gear box, 2 Stromberg 97 carbs.

PHIL WEIAND'S car. '27 'T' body, '42 Merc
engine, Stelling gear box, Weber cam, Weiand
heads & manifold, Scintilla magneto, 3.78 ratio,
Stromberg carburetors.

Car owned by HOWARD JOHANSEN. '24 'T' Roadster, Model 'B' 4-port Riley mill, Howard gear
box, Johansen cam, American-Bosch mag., 3.78
rear end ratio.

VINCE DUARTE'S car. '24 'T' body, Ford 6
engine, Knudsen head, Clay Smith cam, 2 Ford 6
carburetors, standard transmission, 3.54 ratio,
99 in. wheelbase.

CONNIE WIEDELL'S track car. '24 'T' body, Ford 6 mill, Bell gear box, Knudsen head, Smith cam, Knudsen carburetor, stock ignition. Car designed for 'three-quarter' body also.

JIM RATHMAN'S neat job. '27 'T' Roadster, Merc engine, Stelling gear box Weber cam, Weiand heads, 2 Stromberg pots, Weiand manifold, 4.11 to 1 rear end ratio.

TROY RUTTMAN in Dell Baxter's car. '27 'T'
Roadster, '46 Merc, Harman-Collins cam, Offenhauser heads, Chandler-Grove carburetion, Stelling gear box 4.11 to 1 ratio.

One good reason why Wayne Tipton likes to win
Hot Rod races. The car is a '25 'T' rdstr., '39
Merc, Stelling gears, Brumby cam, Offenhauser
heads & Manifold, ratio 3.44. The model is
Betty Laxson of Los Angeles.

ED NEALLY'S track job. '24 'T' body, Ford 6 engine, std. transmission, Clay Smith cam, Knudsen head, Willys steering, 4.11 to 1 rear end ratio.

BUD ZENOR'S No. 38. '29 Model 'A' body, '39 Merc engine, Weber cam, Edelbrock heads, Weiand manifold, Stromberg pots, standard transmission 3.78 to 1 ratio.

PAUL CANTARANO'S car. '22 'T' roadster,
Model 'B' Ford block, Cragar head, Wico magneto,
Harman-Collins cam, Winfield S. R. Carburetor,
Howard gear box, 3.78 to 1 ratio.

MANUEL AYULO'S No. 44. '27 'T' roadster, '41
Merc, Meyers heads & ignition, Evans manifold,
Stelling gear box, Winfield cam, Chandler-Grove
carburetor, 4.11 to 1 ratio.

No. 56 owned by GINO ROSSO. '27 'T' roadster,
'38 V8 mill, Howard gear box, Edelbrock heads &
manifold, Harman-Collins cam, Stromberg 97 carb.
4.11 to 1 ratio.

No. 74 owned by DICK VINEYARD and BOB LINDSAY
'27 'T' roadster, '42 Merc, Winfield super cam,
Edelbrock heads, Evans manifold, std. transmission, Stromberg 97 carb. 4.11 to 1 ratio.

YAM OKA'S No. 105.   '29 'A' body, '40 Merc
engine, Winfield cam, Weiand heads, Edelbrock
manifold, Spalding ignition, 4:33 to 1 ratio.

Difference of opinion as to direction.   Soon
after this picture was taken there was a loud
noise, and, as the cartoon character says from
the movie screen, ''THAT'S ALL, FOLKS''.

CPSIA information can be obtained at www.ICGtesting.com
Printed in the USA
LVOW10s1225011114

411598LV00005B/113/P